THE PLAYBOOK

Emile "Moe" Manara

iUniverse, Inc.
New York   Bloomington

The Playbook

*The views expressed in this work are solely those of the author
and do not necessarily reflect the views of the publisher, and
the publisher hereby disclaims any responsibility for them.
iUniverse books may be ordered through booksellers or by contacting:*

*iUniverse
1663 Liberty Drive
Bloomington, IN 47403
www.iuniverse.com
1-800-Authors (1-800-288-4677)*

*Because of the dynamic nature of the Internet, any Web addresses or
links contained in this book may have changed since publication and
may no longer be valid. The views expressed in this work are solely those
of the author and do not necessarily reflect the views of the publisher,
and the publisher hereby disclaims any responsibility for them.*

*ISBN: 978-1-4401-1724-4 (pbk)
ISBN: 978-1-4401-1725-1 (ebk)*

Printed in the United States of America

iUniverse rev. date: 3/20/2009

To all the exciting women who
lost their place in line. . .

A note from your author:

Very simple, the Playbook is about understanding women, asking the right questions and being man enough to move on when the shine is gone.

All of us alpha males have to accept the fact that women are smarter than us and they know we are basically clueless, ill-equipped and unprepared to deal with their iron curtain of secrecy.

You can read the Playbook in 30 minutes. Or you can take 2 hours or even a few days. Up to you. So, grab a crayon, scribble in the margins, but start now. There will be no table of contents, no chapters, no acknowledgements, no visuals, no mention of a writers' group, no good friends, no family, no editor, no agent. Always remember, there is nothing wrong with a table for one...

AUNT GRACE WAS RIGHT,
TREAT THEM ROUGH AND
TELL THEM NOTHING...

NO MATTER HOW YOU
TRY, SOME MEMORIES
JUST WON'T DIE...

LET'S NOT PRETEND TO BE SOMETHING WE'RE NOT...

THE SHINE WENT AWAY...

UNFORTUNATELY, THE
FANTASY WORLD YOU
CREATED FOR THE TWO
OF YOU DISAPPEARED…

SOME FOOL TOLD ME A
RELATIONSHIP WITHOUT
PAIN IS A RELATIONSHIP
NOT WORTH HAVING...

I INVITED HER INTO
MY WORLD AND SHE
DID NOTHING TO
STAY THERE...

STOP CRYING YOU FOOL, TEARS WON'T TURN INTO ROSES...

YOU WERE SO IN LOVE
YOU COULDN'T SEE
OR KNOW THE RIDE
WAS ALL WRONG...

YOU WERE FOOLISH
ENOUGH TO THINK
YOU COULD MAKE
THE MAGIC LAST...

IN MOST CASES, IT WILL
ALWAYS COME DOWN
TO GOODBYE...

WHEN IT IS OVER, DO
YOU FIND YOURSELF
WONDERING WHERE
DOES THE LOVE GO...

AS YOU LOOK BACK, YOU
CAN NOW SEE THAT
EVERY STEP OF THE
WAY WITH HER WAS
THE WRONG WAY...

YOU ARE NOT A FOOL
FOR CARING, YOU ARE
A FOOL BECAUSE YOU
TOOK HER BACK. SHE
KNOWS IT TOO…

FOR MOST OF US ALPHA
MALES, WE KNOW
THAT GIVING IS THE
SECRET OF LIVING...

REMEMBER, LOVES
DIES BY THE INCH...

WHEN YOU ARE ALONE
WITH YOURSELF, ASK THE
QUESTION, IS THIS THE
LOVE LIFE I ORDERED...

ACCEPT THE FACT
THAT SHE CLOSED THE
DOOR ON YOU...

YOU CAN'T HAVE
ROMANCE WITHOUT
FINANCE. THEY
KNOW IT TOO...

WAKE UP AND SAY
GOODBYE TO YESTERDAY...

LOVE LASTS LONGER THAN
A LIFETIME. THIS IS THE
WISDOM OF A FOOL...

ONLY A FOOL TRIES TO SEE
THROUGH HIS TEARS...

I WASN'T TRYING TO
CONTROL HER LIFE, I
WAS TRYING TO MAKE
OUR LIFE BETTER...

WHY IS IT THAT AT THE
END OF A RELATIONSHIP,
YOU THINK BACK TO
HOW IT STARTED...

DOES SHE HOLD YOUR
HAND? IF NOT, RUN...
DOES SHE ALWAYS
WALK AHEAD OF
YOU? IF YES, RUN...

IS SHE ALWAYS IN A HURRY? IF YES, RUN...

DOES SHE WANT TO COOK FOR YOU? IF NOT, RUN...

WHEN WAS THE LAST TIME SHE CALLED YOU BY YOUR FIRST NAME...

DO YOU ALWAYS HAVE
TO DRIVE, DO YOU
ALWAYS HAVE TO PICK
THE RESTAURANT, DO
YOU ALWAYS HAVE TO PAY,
DO YOU ALWAYS HAVE
TO MAKE EVERYTHING
HAPPEN? IF YES, RUN...

DOES SHE DRIVE AROUND
WITH THE STEREO
BLASTING LISTENING
TO RAP, IF YES, RUN...

IS SHE A FLIRT, IS SHE
HIGH MAINTENANCE,
IS SHE UNGRATEFUL? IF
YOU THINK SO, RUN...
IS SHE ALWAYS ON THE
CELL PHONE TALKING
TO HER GIRLFRIENDS
ABOUT MINDLESS
MATTERS, IF YES, RUN...
LOVE AT GUNPOINT
IS UNACCEPTABLE...

IS SHE RELUCTANT TO
DISCUSS FINANCIAL
MATTERS, OR HER
INVESTMENT PHILOSOPHY
WITH YOU, IF YES, RUN...

IS SHE RELUCTANT TO
DISCUSS A FUTURE WITH
YOU, IF YES, YOU ARE
WASTING YOUR
TIME, RUN...

DOES SHE WEAR AN ANKLE BRACELET. IF YES, RUN…

IS SHE RELUCTANT
TO DISCUSS SUBJECTS
THAT FOREVER COUPLES
NORMALLY DISCUSS,
IF YES, RUN...

DO YOU ALWAYS HAVE TO ENTERTAIN HER? IF YES, RUN...

WHEN WAS THE LAST TIME SHE SURPRISED YOU WITH A BAUBLE OR A KISS?

HOW MANY TATTOOS
DOES SHE HAVE?

HOW MANY TIMES HAS SHE BEEN MARRIED?

HOW MANY ABORTIONS
DID SHE HAVE?

HOW MANY TIMES DID SHE DECLARE BANKRUPTCY?

HOW MANY TIMES
WAS SHE ARRESTED?

IS SHE DRUG DEPENDENT?

DOES SHE DRINK
EVERY DAY?

DOES SHE SMOKE?

IS SHE A RECOVERING ALCOHOLIC?

HOW MANY DOGS AND CATS DOES SHE HAVE?

HOW MANY TIMES
WAS SHE ENGAGED?

HOW MANY TIMES WAS SHE DIVORCED?

HOW MANY CHILDREN DOES SHE HAVE?

HOW MUCH CHILD SUPPORT DOES SHE PAY A MONTH?

DOES SHE OWN HER HOME OR DOES SHE RENT A ROOM WITH SEVERAL STRANGERS?

HOW MANY CREDIT CARDS DOES SHE HAVE?

DOES SHE LIVE BEYOND
HER MEANS? IF YES, RUN…

DOES SHE GO TO LAS VEGAS WITH HER GIRLFRIENDS JUST TO SHOP. IF YES, RUN…

DOES SHE GO TO THE RACE TRACK DURING THE WEEK. IF YES, RUN…

DOES SHE HAVE TO GO
DANCING ONCE A WEEK
TO FEEL GOOD ABOUT
HERSELF. IF YES, RUN...

DOES SHE ALWAYS HAVE TO GO TO THE THEATRE.   IF YES, RUN...

DOES SHE ALWAYS HAVE
TO GO TO A ROCK
CONCERT. IF YES, RUN…
DOES SHE HAVE TO BUY A
PAIR OF SHOES EVERY WEEK
TO FEEL GOOD ABOUT
HERSELF. IF YES, RUN…

DOES SHE INSIST
ON HAVING BREAST
IMPLANTS. IF YES, RUN...

DOES SHE INSIST
ON HAVING BOTOX
INJECTIONS. IF YES, RUN...

DOES SHE INSULT YOU
IN PUBLIC OR IN MIXED
COMPANY. IF YES, RUN…

DOES SHE KNOW HOW
TO CLEAN HOUSE.
IF NOT, RUN…

DOES SHE KNOW HOW TO IRON. IF NOT, RUN...

DOES SHE KNOW HOW TO PURCHASE A CAR. IF NOT, RUN...

ALL WOMEN GRAVITATE TO
FUN AND GOOD TIMES...

YOU MUST ALWAYS
BE THE FUN GUY.

ALL WOMEN HAVE
TEMPORARY DALLIANCES
THAT YOU DO NOT
KNOW ABOUT...

UNFORTUNATELY, IF
YOU DON'T PERFORM
AND PRODUCE FOR
HER, SHE WILL RUN...

THEY ALL HAVE
DOUBTFUL MINDS...

IT IS BETTER TO
WAIT ALONE RATHER
THAN BE USED...

IF SHE TELLS YOU THAT
SHE WILL NEVER BE
FINISHED LOVING
YOU, SHE IS LYING…

SHE COULD CARE LESS
THAT YOUR BROKEN
HEART HAS TURNED
TO STONE...

REMEMBER THIS, THEY ALL HAVE THE CRAZY GENE...

ALPHA MALES DO NOT
LIVE IN CONTINUOUS
FEAR OF BEING HURT...

REMEMBER WHEN THE
HAPPIEST MOMEMTS IN
OUR LIVES WERE WHEN WE
PLAYED LIKE CHILDREN
RATHER THAN COMPETE
FOR THE AFFECTION
OF A WOMAN...

BE A WINNER, BE
POWERFUL, BE FAMOUS,
BE RICH, BE IMPORTANT
FOR YOU, NOT FOR HER...

DOES SHE ALWAYS HAVE TO BE RIGHT, IF YES, RUN...

ALWAYS REMEMBER,
YOU HAVE THE RIGHT
TO BE HAPPY...

ALWAYS REMEMBER,
THE ONE WHO CARES
LEAST ABOUT THE
RELATIONSHIP, CONTROLS
THE RELATIONSHIP...

IF YOU STAY WITH
HER BECAUSE YOU ARE
AFRAID TO BE ALONE,
YOU ARE A FOOL…

YOUR HAPPINESS
SHOULD COME FROM
YOU, NEVER HER…
DOES SHE SAY YOU ANNOY
HER, DOES SHE SAY SHE IS
ASHAMED OF YOU, DOES
SHE SAY YOU EMBARRASS
HER. IF YES, GET OUT
NOW. THE RELATIONSHIP
IS DOOMED…

REMEMBER, WHEN YOU
MAKE A MISTAKE WITH
HER, YOU PAY ONLY ONCE
FOR THAT MISTAKE...

WHY NOT GET WHAT
YOU WANT IN LIFE.
DON'T WASTE YOUR
TIME OR HERS.

YOU BETTER KNOW
WHAT YOU WANT IN
LIFE. DON'T INVENT
WHAT IS NOT THERE...

DOES SHE OWN HER OWN WASHER AND DRYER. IF NOT, RUN...

IS SHE STILL USING
THE COIN OPERATED
LAUNDROMAT. IF
YES, RUN…

IF SHE IS AN ATTRACTIVE
WOMAN, THERE IS ALWAYS
SOMEONE ELSE...
IS SHE IN A RELATIONSHIP
WITH YOU BECAUSE SHE
WANTS TO HAVE FUN...

IS SHE IN A RELATIONSHIP
WITH YOU BECAUSE
SHE WANTS TO SHARE
EVERYTHING WITH YOU...

IS SHE IN A RELATIONSHIP
WITH YOU BECAUSE SHE
IS BORED WITH HER
PREVIOUS RELATIONSHIP...

THE ONLY IMPORTANT MISSION IN LIFE IS TO MAKE YOURSELF HAPPY...

DO YOU LIKE THE WAY
YOU LOOK. DO YOU
LIKE YOURSELF THE
WAY YOU ARE...

IF YOU DON'T HAVE
LOVE, IT'S BECAUSE YOU
DON'T LOVE YOURSELF...

ALL BEAUTIFUL WOMEN
HAVE POWER OVER
MEN. SO, DON'T LET
HER CONTROL YOU...

SHE CAN NOT SHARE
WITH YOU WHAT SHE
DOES NOT HAVE...

THE REASON YOU WERE PLACED HERE ON EARTH WAS TO HAVE FUN...

SOONER OR LATER,
WE MEN ARE FOOLED
BY A PRETTY FACE...

WHY IS IT THAT A
MAN IS EXPECTED TO
ALWAYS BE RESPONSIBLE
FOR FULFILLING A
WOMANS NEEDS...

LOVE KEEPS NO RECORDS
OF RIGHTS AND WRONGS.
DON'T BELIEVE IT...
LOVE NEVER FAILS.
DON'T BELIEVE IT...

LOVE IS KIND. DON'T BELIEVE IT...

LOVE IS PATIENT.
DON'T BELIEVE IT...

WHEN WAS THE LAST TIME SHE TOLD YOU HOW HANDSOME YOU ARE...

WHEN WAS THE LAST
TIME SHE TOLD YOU HOW
PROUD SHE IS OF YOU...

WHEN WAS THE LAST TIME SHE SURPRISED YOU WITH AN AMBUSH KISS...

WHEN WAS THE LAST TIME SHE HELD YOUR HAND IN PUBLIC...

TOLERATING WELL IS
NOT LIVING WELL...

DID SHE EVER ASK YOU WHAT YOUR BIGGEST WEAKNESS IS...

DID SHE EVER ASK YOU
WHAT YOUR GREATEST
STRENGTH IS...
DID SHE EVER ASK YOU
WHAT YOUR GREATEST
PLEASURES IN LIFE ARE...

DID YOU KNOW THAT
FORGIVENESS IS NOT
A ONE-TIME EVENT...

DOES SHE CARE FOR
YOU THE WAY YOU
CARE FOR HER...

YOU ARE NOT OBLIGATED TO TELL HER EVERYTHING...

DOES SHE UNDERSTAND
THAT AN INTIMATE
CONVERSATION WITH
YOU CANNOT INCLUDE
AN ARGUMENT...
WHAT HAS SHE
CONTIBUTED TO YOUR
LOVE-FILLED LASTING
RELATIONSHIP...

REMIND HER THAT HEART-TO-HEART TALKS DON'T HAPPEN ON THE GO...

DOES SHE GAB ABOUT
THE GOOD...

DOES SHE MAKE
YOU LAUGH...

DOES SHE TALK IN FOREVER TERMS...

**DOES SHE THINK IN
FOREVER TERMS...
DOES SHE LOVE YOU
BECAUSE SHE NEEDS YOU...**

DOES SHE NEED YOU
BECAUSE SHE LOVES YOU...

MOST ALPHA MALES
THINK TOUCHING IS THE
BEST WAY OF SPEAKING
TO YOUR PARTNER…

DOES SHE BRAG
ABOUT YOU...

NOTHING CAN WARM-UP A NEGLECTED MAN...

ALPHA MALES ARE NOT MIND READERS...

IT'S THE LITTLE THINGS THAT REALLY MATTER...

TOUCHING IS THE PRIMARY LANGUAGE OF LOVE...

ALPHA MALES DO NOT HUNT FOR TRAGEDY...

YOUR DUTY AS AN
ALPHA MALE DOES NOT
HAVE TO BE DULL...
WHAT KILLS ROMANCE
IS SAMENESS...

DOES SHE WEAR A TOE RING. IF YES, RUN...

DOES SHE WEAR A THUMB
RING. IF YES, RUN NOW...

HOW MANY RINGS AND THINGS DOES SHE WEAR ON EACH HAND...

REMEMBER, SOMEONE HAD YOUR JOB BEFORE YOU…

REMEMBER, SOMEONE WILL HAVE YOUR JOB AFTER YOU...

REMEMBER, YOU HAVE THE JOB NOW, SO, ENJOY IT...

THE MORE YOU GIVE THEM, THE MORE THEY EXPECT...

NEVER GET INVOLVED
WITH A WOMAN UNLESS
SHE CAN GIVE BACK TO
THE RELATIONSHIP AT THE
LEVEL THAT YOU GIVE...

DON'T BE AN EXPERT AT
NOT ACCEPTING THE
TRUTH-WHEN IT'S OVER-
WALK AWAY, FOREVER...

DON'T LET THEM
CHANGE YOUR WAY OF
DRESSING, YOUR WAY
OF COMBING YOUR
HAIR, YOUR FRAGRANCE,
YOUR WAY OF EATING,
YOUR WAY OF LIFE…

WOMEN CAN SPOT A DESPERATE MAN AT FIFTY METERS...

IF SHE SPENDS LOTS OF
TIME DOING SODUKO
AND CROSSWORD
PUZZLES, RUN AWAY AS
FAST AS POSSIBLE…

FACE IT, YOU ARE WHO
YOU ARE AND NOT WHAT
SHE WANTS YOU TO BE...

DON'T BE A FOOL
AND THINK YOU
LOVED HER FIRST...

DON'T BE A FOOL AND
THINK YOU LOVED
HER THE BEST...

BE HONEST, IS SHE
REALLY GIVING YOU HER
BEST? IF NOT, RUN...

ARE THERE TIMES WHEN SHE ENJOYS PUNISHING YOU? IF YES, RUN...

IF YOU ARE SUFFERING
IN YOUR RELATIONSHIP
WITH HER, IT'S BECAUSE
YOU CHOOSE TO SUFFER...

SUFFERING, LIKE HAPPINESS, IS A CHOICE...

CAN YOU IMAGINE LIVING
EVERYDAY WITHOUT THE
FEAR OF BEING REJECTED...

DOES SHE HAVE THE NEED TO MAKE YOU WRONG...

DOES SHE LIVE HER
LIFE WITH HER EYES
CLOSED. IF YES, RUN…

YOU WERE BORN WITH THE RIGHT TO BE HAPPY...

SAY NO WHEN YOU
WANT TO SAY NO, SAY YES
WHEN YOU WANT TO SAY
YES. BE A REAL MAN...

DOES SHE HAVE A
NEED FOR ATTENTION.
IF YES, RUN...
FACE IT, IT'S TIME TO
PAY FOR PICKING THE
WRONG ONE...

FACE THE TRUTH, NO MORE TABLE FOR TWO...

REMEMBER, YOU CAN'T BE
ON STAGE EVERY NIGHT...

THEY SAY A DEAD MAN IS
HEAVIER THAN A BROKEN
HEART. DON'T BELIEVE IT...

NOT EVEN YOU CAN MAKE
ALL OF YOUR DREAMS
COME TRUE. WELCOME
TO THE REAL WORLD...

ONCE A WOMAN CAME
INTO OUR LIVES,
RUNNING THE BASES
WAS NEVER THAT MUCH
FUN EVER AGAIN...

IS SHE YOUR FULL INTELLECTUAL EQUAL. IF NOT, RUN...

THE HIDDEN TRUTH
IS THAT MOST WOMEN
DON'T   CARE OR
WANT TO GIVE
BACK TO THE
RELATIONSHIP...

DO YOU GO TO BED EVERY
NIGHT THINKING HOW
YOU CAN MAKE HER
HAPPIER. IF YES, STOP IT...

DO YOU WAKE UP EACH
MORNING THINKING
HOW YOU CAN MAKE HER
HAPPIER. IF YES, STOP IT...

IF SHE SAYS HER MALE
FRIENDS ARE ALL GAY,
SHE IS LYING TO YOU...

REMEMBER, WHAT'S MOST
IMPORTANT IS WHO YOU
ARE WITH RATHER THAN
WHAT YOU ARE DOING...

NEVER SETTLE...

YOU TREAT HER LIKE
YOUR QUEEN. DOES SHE
TREAT YOU LIKE HER
KING. IF NOT, RUN...

DID SHE SELECT YOU AND
THEN DESELECT YOU AS
HER PERSONAL NEEDS
CHANGED. A PRETTY FACE
WILL DO THAT TO YOU...

YOU NEVER HEAR FROM
THEM UNLESS THEY
NEED SOMETHING...
WE ALPHA MALES HAVE
NO DEFENSE AGAINST
A PRETTY FACE AND
THEY KNOW THIS...

UNFORTUNATELY, WE
CAN'T LIVE WITH THEM
AND WE CAN'T LIVE
WITHOUT THEM. THEY
KNOW THIS TOO...